SCHIRMER'S LIBRARY
OF MUSICAL CLASSICS

Vol. 2070

CLAUDE DEBUSSY

Favorite Piano Works

ISBN 978-1-4234-2741-4

G. SCHIRMER, Inc.

DISTRIBUTED BY

 HAL•LEONARD®
CORPORATION

7777 W. BLUEMOUND RD. P.O. BOX 13819 MILWAUKEE, WI 53213

CONTENTS

4   About the Composer

Children's Corner
5   I. Doctor Gradus ad Parnassum
10   II. Jimbo's Lullaby
14   III. Serenade for the Doll
20   IV. The Snow is Dancing
26   V. The Little Shepherd
28   VI. Golliwogg's Cake-walk

Deux arabesques
33   Arabesque No. 1
38   Arabesque No. 2

Estampes
45   Pagodes
53   La soirée dans Grenade
59   Jardins sous la pluie

69   Hommage à Haydn

Images
Set I
73   Reflets dans l'eau
80   Hommage à Rameau
85   Mouvement
Set II
97   Cloches à travers les feuilles
104 Et la lune descend sur le temple qui fût
109 Poissons d'or

122 L'isle joyeuse

141 Masques

136   Le petit nègre

156   La plus que lente

from *Préludes, Book 1*
162   VI. Des pas sur la neige
164   VIII. La fille aux cheveux de lin
166   X. La Cathédrale engloutie
171   XII. Minstrels

from *Préludes, Book 2*
175   III. La Puerta del vino

179   Rêverie

Suite bergamasque
185   Prélude
191   Menuet
198   Clair de lune
204   Passepied

Suite: Pour le piano
213   Prélude
224   Sarabande
228   Toccata

Claude Debussy
(1862–1918)

Claude Debussy was one of the most brilliant and important composers of the late-19th and early-20th centuries. His compositions had a profound effect on the composers that followed him, particularly owing to a new style of music that he helped create along with his contemporary, Maurice Ravel. Debussy developed his own sonic palette in his piano and orchestral compositions, rejecting much of the prevailing musical theoretical teachings of his day. He famously debated his teacher at the Paris Conservatoire, Ernest Guiraud, saying, "There is no theory. You merely have to listen. Pleasure is the law." (Lockspeiser, *Debussy: His Life and Mind*.) Characteristics of the style he developed included tonal centers rather than clear key associations, the use of whole-tone and other exotic scales, prolific use of parallel chords, and a deliberate ambiguity of rhythm, or lack of a clear rhythmic pulse. The impressionist movement in music implied generous reference to literature and art within musical compositions, exemplified by the many fancifully titled instrumental works by Debussy such as the *Préludes*, *Estampes* and *Images* for piano. (The *Préludes* contain poetic titles curiously printed at the conclusion of each piece.)

The term impressionism was first used (derogatorily) in reference to French art, particularly the style of Claude Monet. In his music, Debussy was profoundly influenced by the "impressionist" painters and also the "symbolist" school of writers, including Paul Verlaine, Arthur Rimbaud, Maurice Maeterlinck, and Charles Baudelaire. Both terms are challenged by modern scholars as offering incomplete views of Debussy's style, and the composer himself disliked the term "impressionist." Other influences on the composer included the music of both Richard Wagner and Debussy's teacher, César Franck, as well as the Javanese music that Debussy heard at the Paris Universal Exhibition in 1889.

Debussy was trained as a pianist, but was not considered to be an outstanding player by the faculty at the Paris Conservatoire where he studied, so he did not pursue a concert career. He wrote music for the piano throughout his life, and ironically contributed some of the most important French works in the modern concert repertoire, as well as a proliferation of student pieces. His evolution as a composer may be traced in these piano pieces.

In this collection, the *Deux arabesques* (1888) and *Rêverie* (1890) are both early pieces, romantic in style, that reveal the influence of visual art on the composer. The *Suite bergamasque* (1890-1905) and *Suite: Pour le Piano* (1896-1901) both recall Baroque dance suites (Menuet, Passepied, Sarabande), revealing Debussy's fondness for retrospective reference to ancient musical styles. The *Estampes* (1903), *L'isle joyeuse* (1904), *Masques* (1904), and the two sets of *Images* (1905, 1907) are collectively some of Debussy's most brilliant works for piano, and are generally considered impressionist in style. Of these, *Masques* and *L'isle joyeuse* were originally conceived as part of a triptych. The *Children's Corner* (1906-08) is a collection of colorfully named short pieces. The *Hommage à Haydn* (1909) is a slow waltz, and *Le petit nègre* (1909) of the same year is a fanciful character piece. *La plus que lente* (1910) is a slow, humorous waltz that the composer also adapted for full orchestra. Finally, our collection includes some of the most famous selections from the *Préludes, Book 1* (1909-10) and *Préludes, Book 2* (1912-13).

—Susanne Sheston

CHILDREN'S CORNER
I. Doctor Gradus ad Parnassum

Claude Debussy
(1862–1918)

Animato ma non troppo

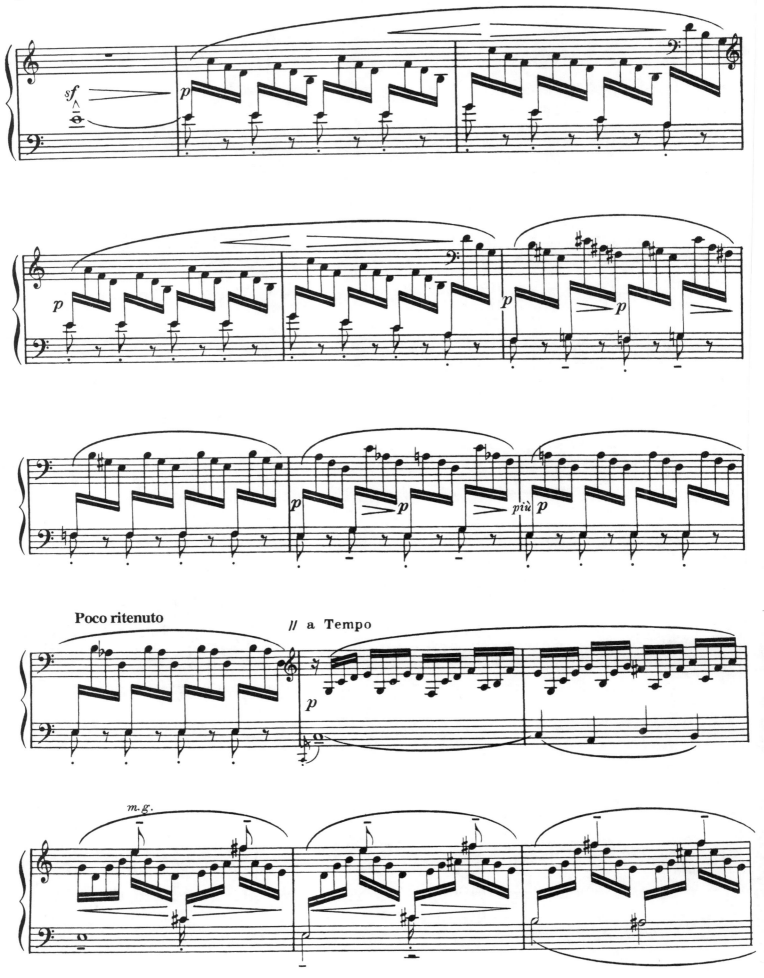

Molto animato

II. Jimbo's Lullaby

III. Serenade for the Doll

Rallentare

più **p**

a Tempo

pp

pp

p *espressivo*

Poco animando

p

p

Tempo I

IV. The Snow is Dancing

21

Poco rallentare

A tempo

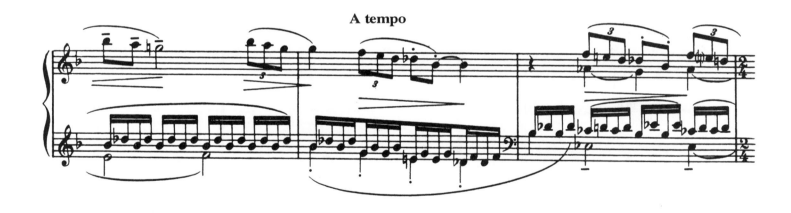

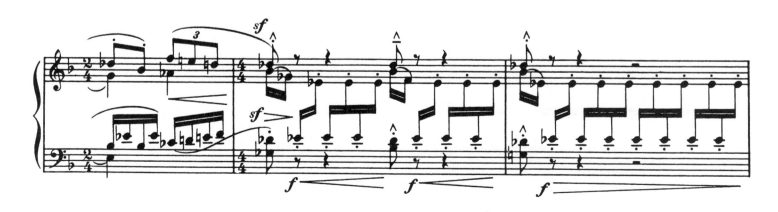

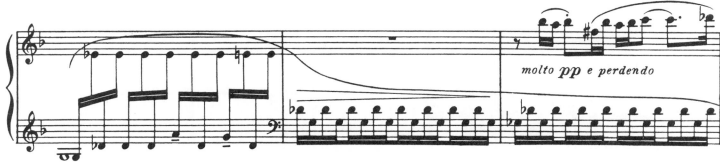

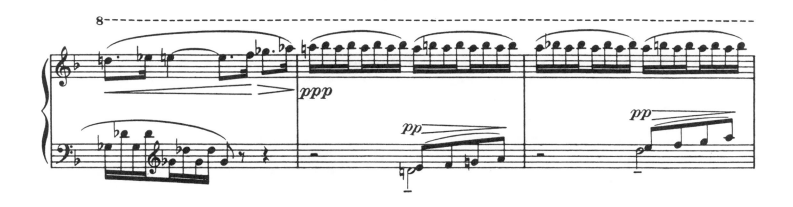

V. The Little Shepherd

VI. Golliwogg's Cake-walk

Poco meno mosso

DEUX ARABESQUES
Arabesque No. 1

Claude Debussy
(1862–1918)

Tempo rubato *(un peu moins vite)* *(somewhat slower)*

Arabesque No. 2

Allegretto scherzando

44

ESTAMPES
Pagodes

Claude Debussy
(1862–1918)

La soirée dans Grenade

Movimento di Habanera

Cominciare lento, in ritmo grazioso e disinvolto

Leggero e lontano
(♩ = ♪ of the preceding measure)

Jardins sous la pluie

Netto e vivo

Calmandosi

Tempo 1 (con meno rigore)

Tempo   animando fin' alla fine

HOMMAGE À HAYDN

Claude Debussy
(1862–1918)

IMAGES
Reflets dans l'eau

Andantino molto
(Tempo rubato)

Claude Debussy
(1862–1918)

in relief

A tempo

mf cresc. molto

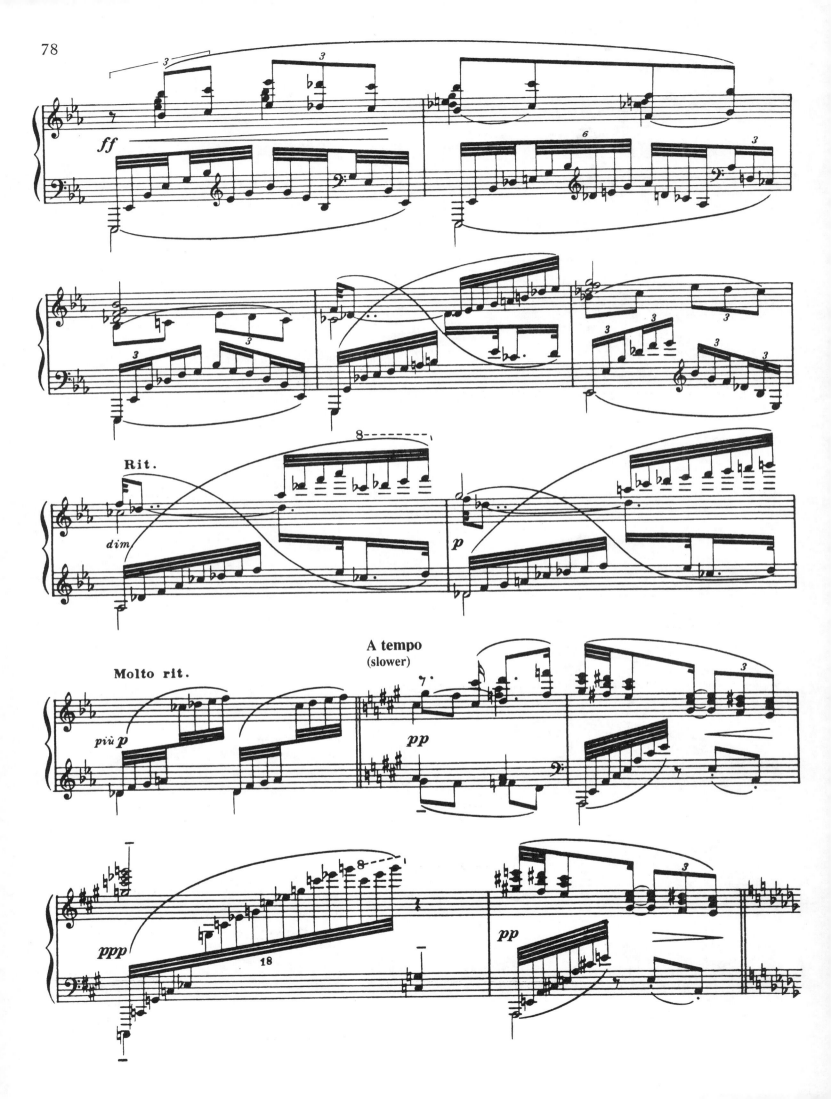

Tempo 1 (slowing down from here to the end)

Hommage à Rameau

Slow and grave
(in the style of a Sarabande, but without stiffness)

Begin slightly below tempo

Mouvement

Animato (with capricious but accurate lightness)

*Notes marked – should be sonorous but without hardness,
the other notes very light but without dryness.*

slightly in relief

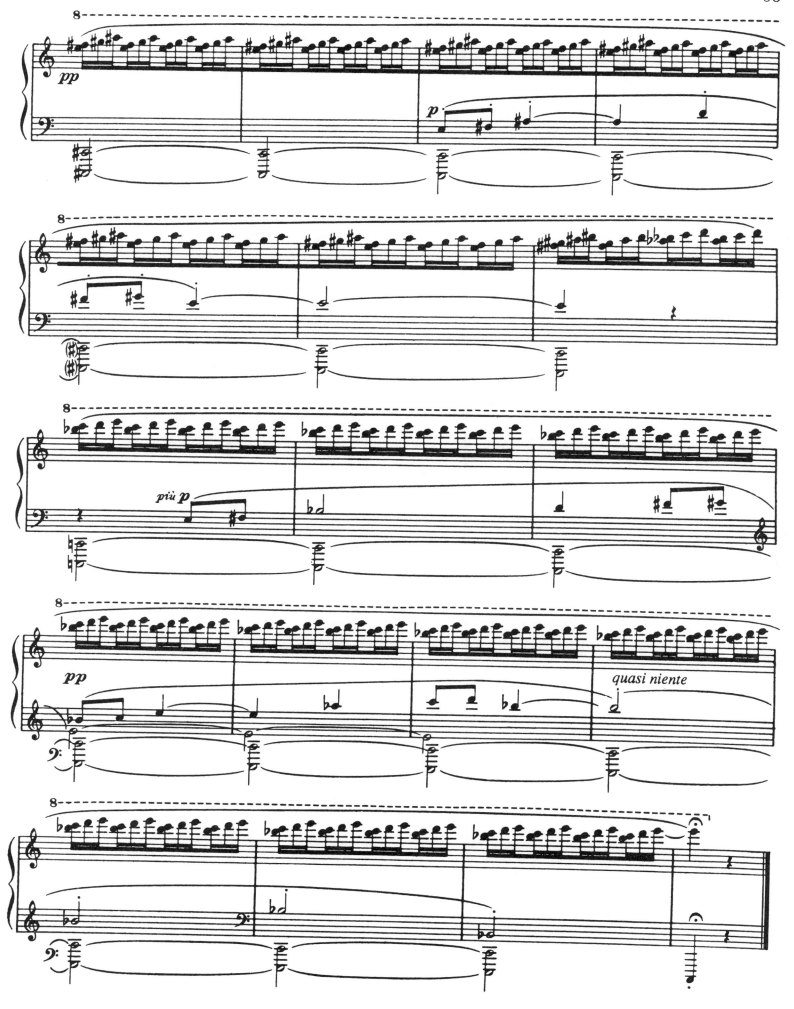

(This page has been intentionally left blank.)

Cloches à travers les feuilles

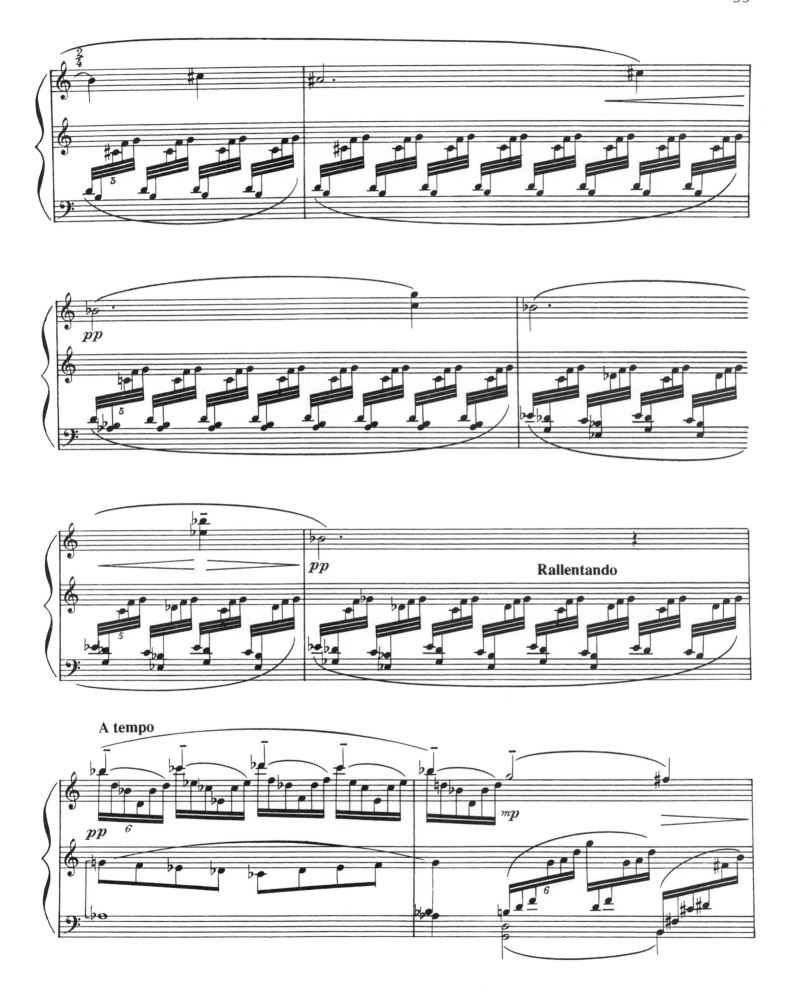

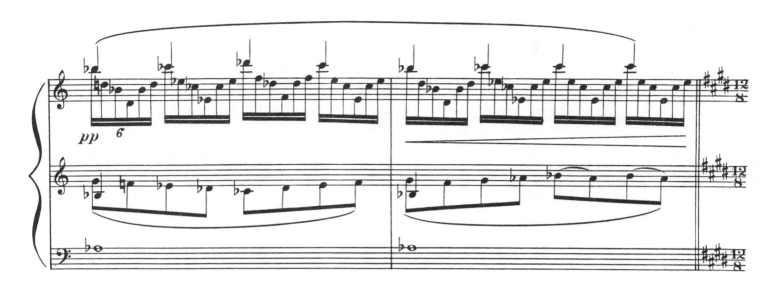

Poco animato; brighter

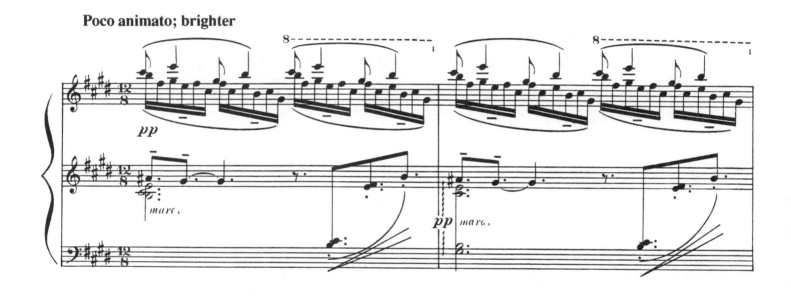

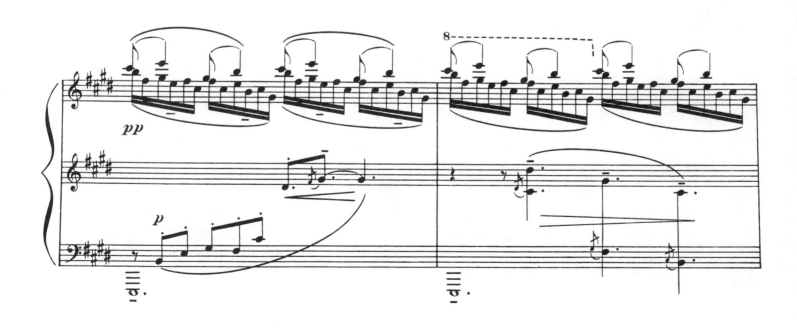

104

Et la lune descend sur le temple qui fût

Poissons d'or

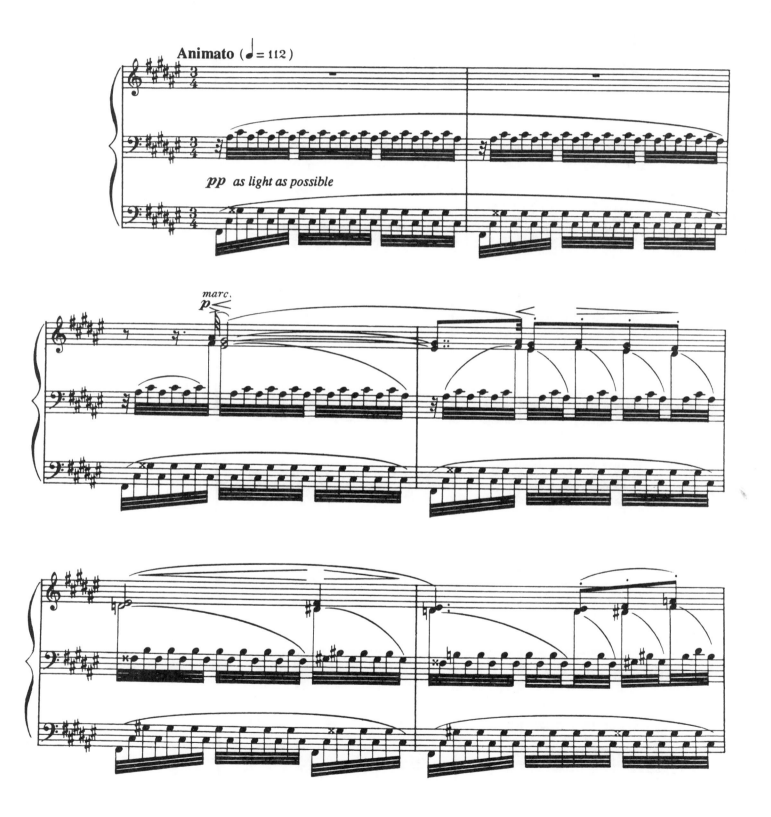

Rallentando

Espressivo and without stiffness

A tempo

Accelerando

As before (espressivo and without stiffness)

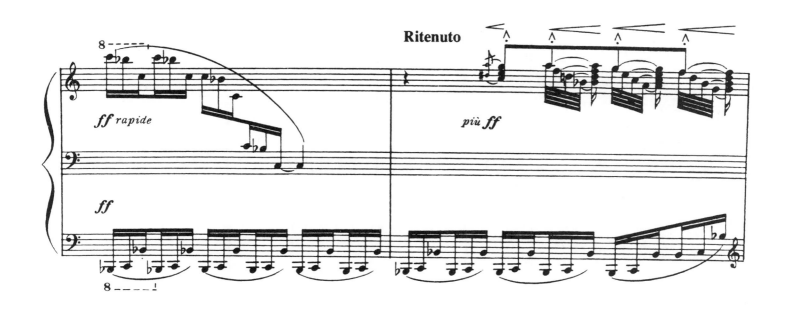

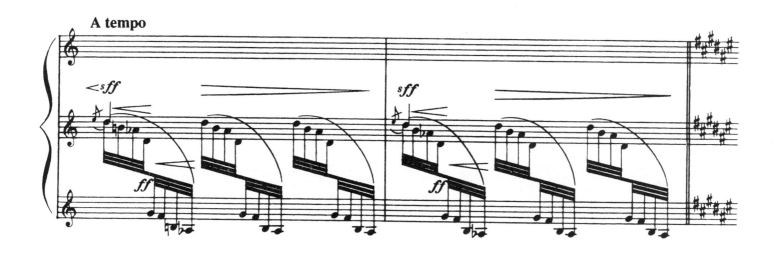

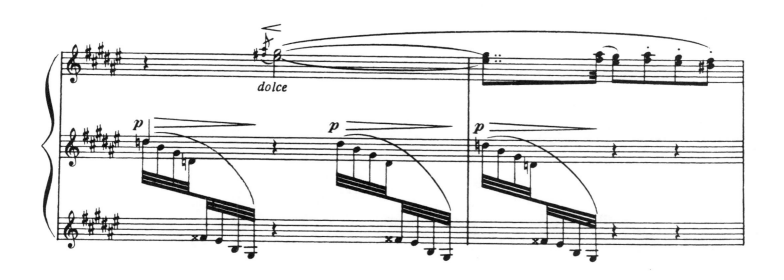

Calming down

Rallentando

Begin below tempo

L'ISLE JOYEUSE

Claude Debussy
(1862–1918)

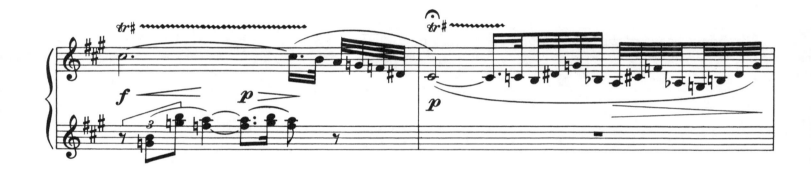

un peu en dehors
(somewhat marked)

Un peu cédé. Molto rubato
(Somewhat slower)

133

LE PETIT NÈGRE

Claude Debussy
(1862–1918)

ritenuto

a Tempo

a Tempo

a Tempo

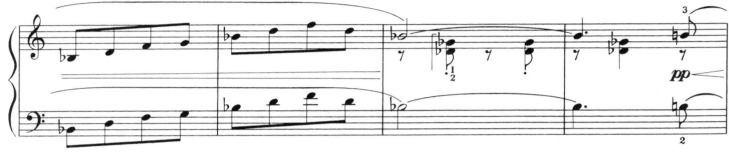

a Tempo

MASQUES

Claude Debussy
(1862–1918)

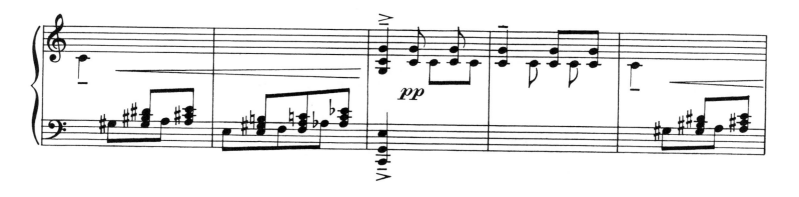

la basse en dehors (emphasize bass)

cédez un peu *(a little slower)*

laissez vibrer pendant ces 4 mesures

LA PLUS QUE LENTE

Claude Debussy
(1862–1918)

VI...
from PRÉLUDES, BOOK 1

Claude Debussy
(1862–1918)

(...Des pas sur la neige)

VIII...
from PRÉLUDES, BOOK 1

Claude Debussy
(1862–1918)

Très calme et doucement expressif (♩=66)

(...La fille aux cheveux de lin)

X...
from PRÉLUDES, BOOK 1

Claude Debussy
(1862–1918)

Profondément calme (Dans une brume doucement sonore)

*) **Doux et fluide**

pp

pp (sans nuances)

*) Debussy, in his piano-roll recording (Welte-Mignon), played measures 7–12 and 22–83 in double speed.

Peu à peu sortant de la brume

Augmentez progressivement (Sans presser)

Sonore sans dureté

Un peu moins lent (Dans une expression allant grandissant)

(...La Cathédrale engloutie)

XII...
from PRÉLUDES, BOOK 1

Claude Debussy
(1862–1918)

Modéré (Nerveux et avec humour)

p les "gruppetti" sur le temps

Cédéz _ // Mouvement

Cédéz _ // Mouvement (Un peu plus allant)

(très détaché)

(...Minstrels)

III...
from PRÉLUDES, BOOK 2

Claude Debussy
(1862–1918)

Mouvement de Habanera
avec de brusques oppositions d'extrême
violence et de passionnée douceur

(...La Puerta del vino)

RÊVERIE

Claude Debussy
(1862–1918)

(This page has been intentionally left blank.)

SUITE BERGAMASQUE
Prélude

Claude Debussy
(1862–1918)

Moderato *(tempo rubato)*

Menuet

Clair de lune

Passepied

cédez un peu
(a little slower)

a tempo

(This page has been intentionally left blank.)

SUITE: POUR LE PIANO
Prélude

Edited by Gaby Casadesus

Claude Debussy
(1862–1918)

Assez animé et très rythmé (Quite lively and very rhythmic)

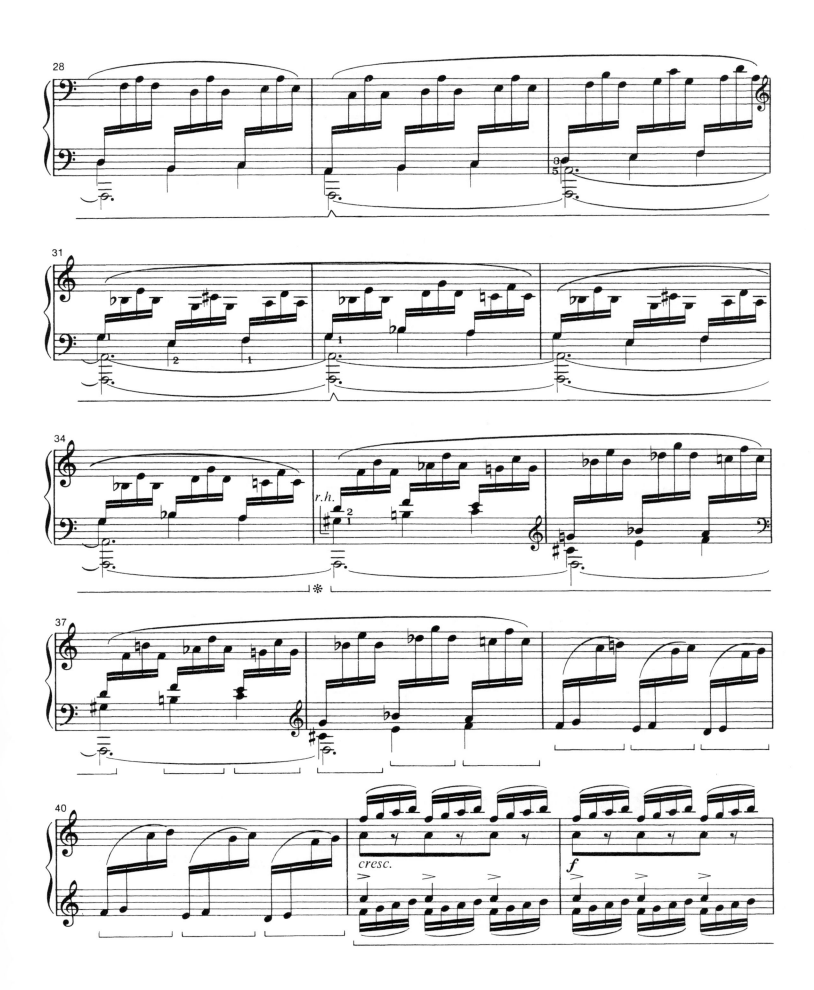

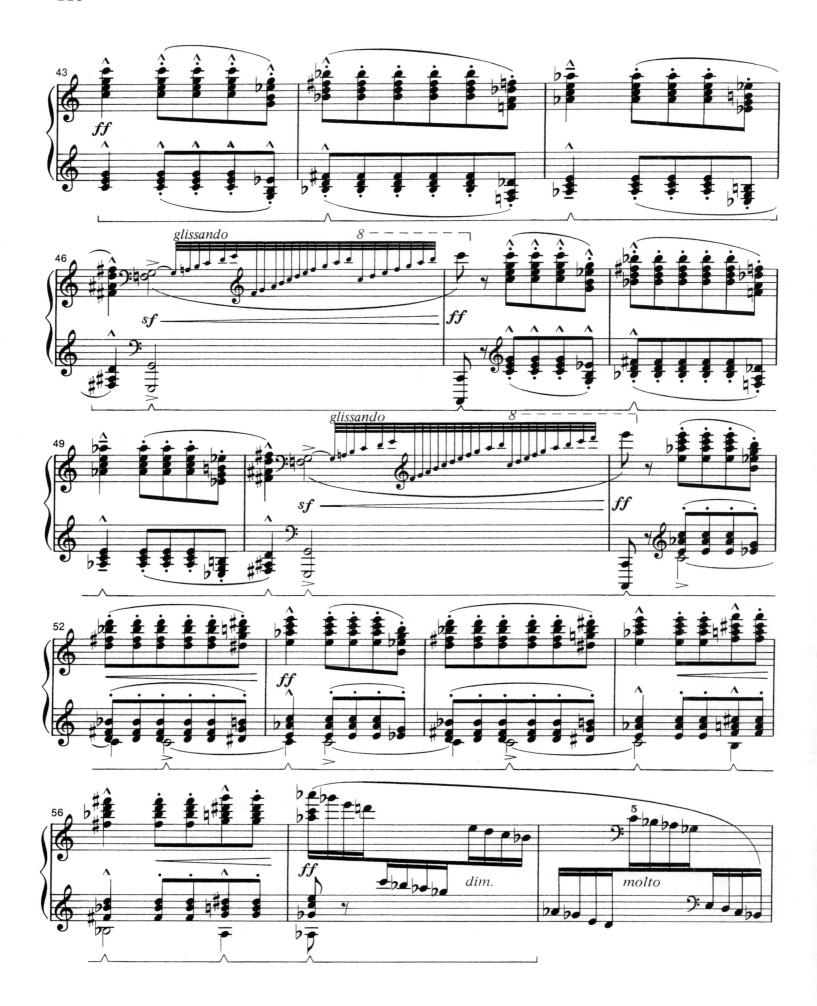

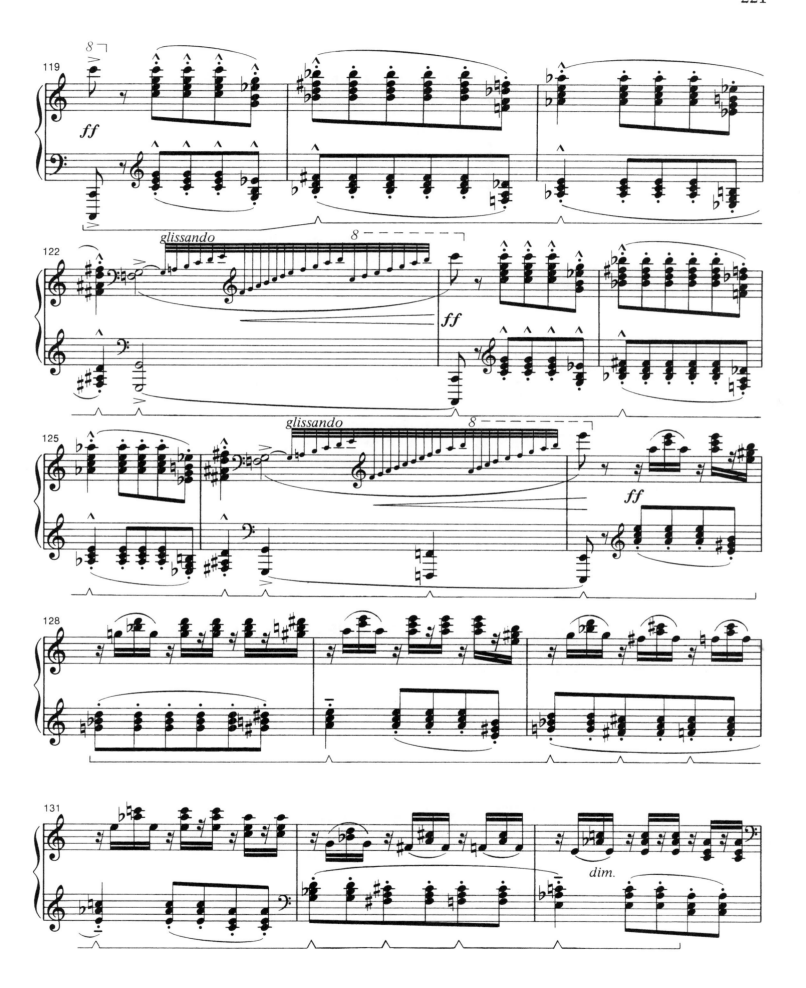

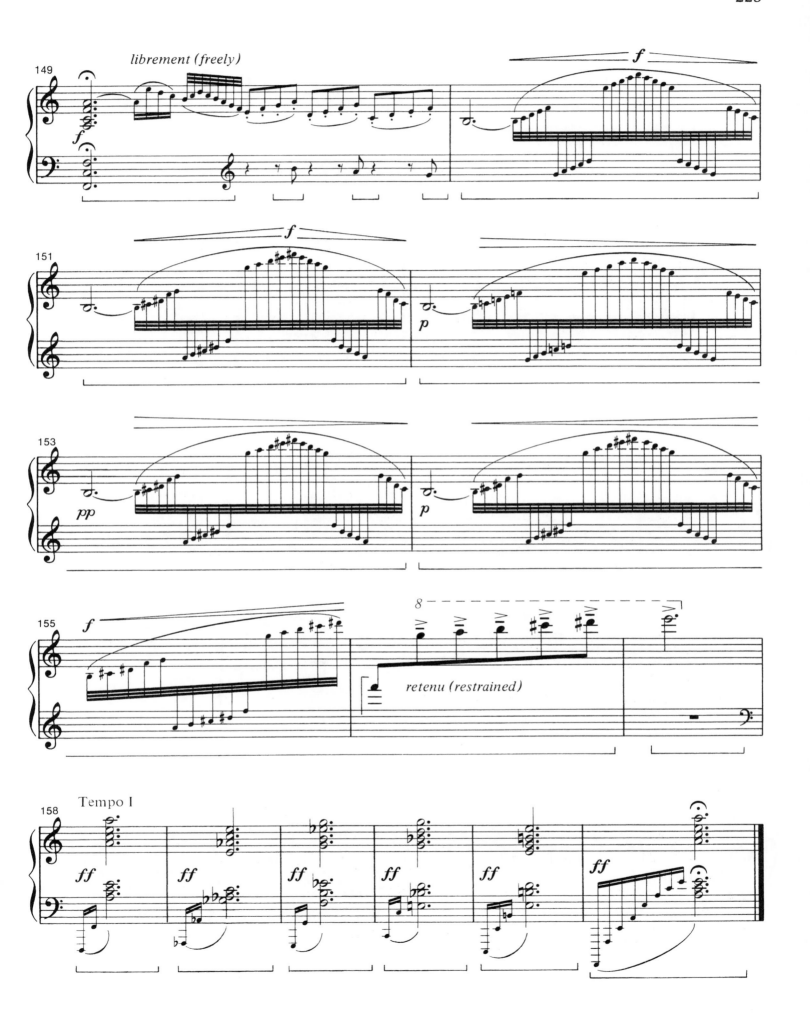

Sarabande

Toccata

230

* arrangement pour petite mains (arrangement for small hands)

232

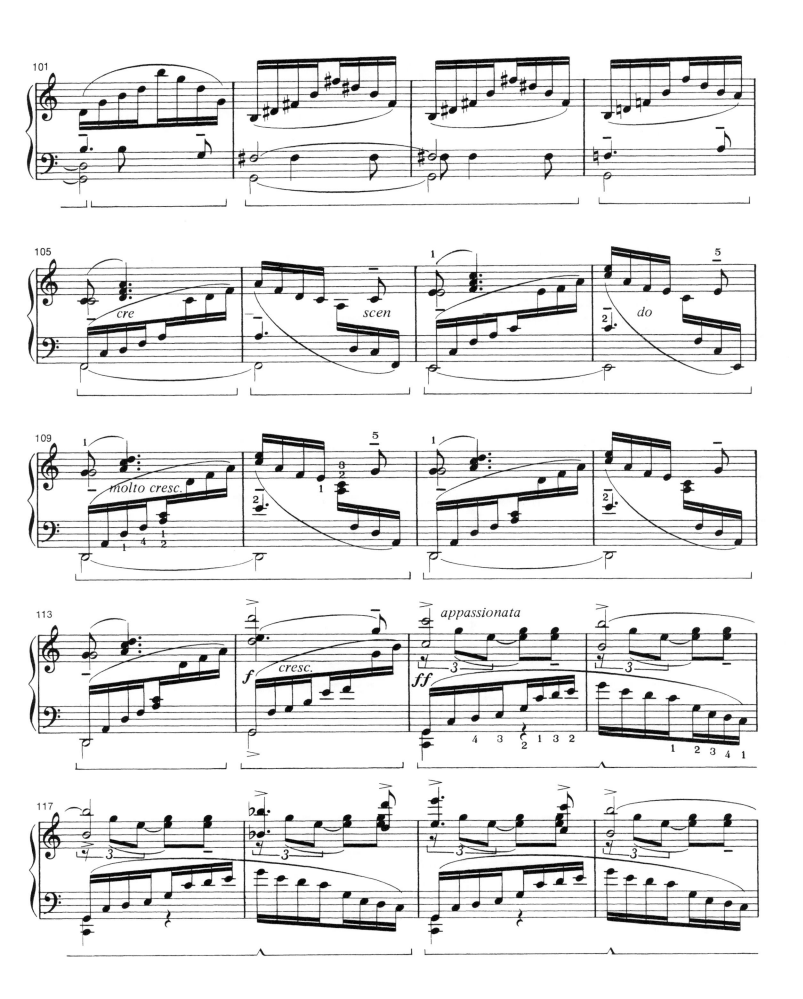